THE

LITTLE

BOOK

OF

BOWL

FOOD

THE LITTLE

BOOK OF

BOWL FOOD

Simple and nourishing recipes in a bowl

Photography by Issy Croker

Hardie Grant

QUADRILLE

Text is extracted and updated from Nourish Bowls, by Quadrille.

Quadrille
52–54 Southwark Street
London
SE1 1UN
quadrille.com

This edition published in 2023 by Quadrille,
an imprint of Hardie Grant Publishing

Text, design, and layout © Quadrille 2016, 2023
Photography © Issy Croker 2016

ISBN 978 1 83783 027 5

Printed In China

INTRODUCTION

Bowl food is made from the heart – comforting, fulfilling, and delicious. It is everything you need in just one bowl to nourish your body and mind, whether you have a few minutes to pull together a meal, want to try out new ingredients and flavours, or help your body recover optimally after a workout.

Cultures all over the world have traditional bowl-based recipes. And now it has become a simple way to bring together a nourishing meal, including all the key nutritional elements, to hold in our hands, however hectic our lives. Putting together the bowl feels like an act of mindfulness in itself, combining natural, flavourful ingredients, textures and colours, vibrancy, and vitality.

Bowl food can be quick and simple to prepare, with many of the elements being included raw. There is so much variety possible, with countless wholesome combinations of vegetables, greens, grains, plant-based proteins, meat, or fish. From breakfast bowls that combine pear with kale in a smoothie served with cinnamon granola, or miso oats with spinach and a poached egg, to a citrus and fennel salad bowl with goat cheese and toasted quinoa, and hearty bowls like mushroom rye risotto with baby chard and walnuts, or chilli chicken with corn and avocado salsa, black quinoa, and zesty sour cream, we hope to give you plenty of inspiration for creating your own flavoursome bowls.

Go bold with your flavours and combinations, layer up your grains, protein, and leafy greens, then scatter over a few toasted seeds, roasted sweet potato crisps, or a little turmeric dressing. Whether you keep it simple with some roasted veggies, homemade hummus, salad leaves, and a few alfalfa sprouts, or fancy some smoked fish with lentils and a big bunch of greens, thinking about the simple elements of the bowl will deliver a nutrient-packed meal every time.

Over the seasons, you can adapt your bowls to the ingredients nature provides. During the summer, add more raw vegetables and leaves, while in the colder months roasted root vegetables are the perfect addition with a red lentil hummus or smashed avocado with lime. There is an amazing variety of grains now available to suit any bowl, especially in your local health food store, including different coloured quinoa, buckwheat, freekeh, millet, and various 'groats', which are the whole grains of foods we might be more used to seeing as flour or flakes, such as oat and rye groats. These add so much variety of taste and texture. There are also lots of seeds in all different sizes, from the tiny chia to flax, sesame, hemp, and pumpkin.

You might find some of the recipes are a little more creative than others, for when you want to try something new and adventurous. There are lots of ideas for elements that you can make ahead and keep handy in the refrigerator, such as dressings, pickles, and pastes. Don't feel you have to bake your own soda bread or make your own ricotta, we have simply included as many recipes as possible for when you might fancy giving these things a try. In most instances, the recipes make enough for one serving. If you want to share a bowl with friends, then multiply the quantities by the number of servings required.

The basic concept of bowl food is to include all the nutritional elements you ideally need in one meal: protein (whether it be plant-based, dairy, fish, or meat), seasonal fruits or vegetables, leafy greens, complex carbohydrates, healthy fats, and any optional extras you fancy like a dressing, a few nuts, or seeds. Let your imagination go.

PROTEIN
aim for approximately
20 to 25 per cent of your bowl
to be made up by protein

VEGETABLES & FRUIT
vegetables, fruits, or
a combination of the two,
should form the largest
proportion of your bowl

LEAFY GREENS
Include a large handful of
leafy greens in every bowl

COMPLEX CARBOHYDRATES
ensure that healthy carbs occupy
approximately 25 per cent of
your bowl

HEALTHY FATS
whenever possible, make
approximately 10 per cent of
your bowl include a healthy fat

TOPPINGS & DRESSINGS
add any optional toppings and
dressings to add extra bite
or flavour

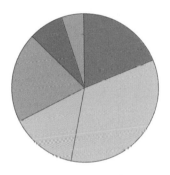

● **PROTEINS**

Protein is a key building block for our muscles, bones, cartilage, skin, and blood. It helps our body carry out all the day-to-day general repair work, especially when we have an active lifestyle. Protein also keeps us fuller for longer as it takes the body more time and effort to break down its nutrients. There are plenty of plant-based proteins to choose from, as well as dairy, eggs, meat, and fish.

PLANT-BASED
- Tofu
- Beans (including aduki, borlotti, broad or fava, edamame, mung, and soybeans)
- Lentils and pulses (including beluga lentils, split peas, green or Puy lentils, and chickpeas /garbanzo beans)
- Quinoa
- Nuts
- Seeds

DAIRY
- Cheese (including goat and sheep cheese)
- Yogurt
- Labneh
- Kefir

FISH AND SHELLFISH
- Cod (use sustainable wherever possible)
- Crab
- Crayfish
- Haddock
- Sea bass
- Mackerel
- Mussels
- Prawns (shrimp)
- Salmon
- Squid
- Trout

ANIMAL SOURCES
- Eggs
- Meat (including chicken, turkey, duck lamb, pork, beef – use organic wherever possible)
- Game birds (including quail and pheasant)

Add extra colour and nutrients to your bowl with whatever veggies or fruits you fancy. You might want to add slices of citrus fruit to your salad bowl, or some grated raw carrot, cucumber ribbons, shredded or fermented cabbage.

VEGETABLES

- Asparagus
- Aubergine (eggplant)
- Beetroot (beet)
- Brassicas (including broccoli, sprouts, cauliflower, and kohlrabi)
- Capsicum (including bell pepper and chilli pepper)
- Carrot
- Celeriac (celery root)
- Courgette (zucchini)
- Cucumber
- Jerusalem artichoke
- Legumes (including peas and mangetout)
- Onion
- Radish
- Samphire
- Sea vegetables (including sea spaghetti, nori flakes, sea salad)
- Spring onion (scallion)
- Squash (including butternut and pumpkin)
- Tomato

FRUITS

- Apple
- Banana
- Berries (including açaí, blackberries, blueberries, loganberries, raspberries, and strawberries)
- Citrus (including clementine, grapefruit and orange)
- Grapes
- Melon
- Pear
- Watermelon

MUSHROOMS

In a group of their own, mushrooms are thought to be particularly beneficial to health.

- Enoki
- Girolle
- Oyster
- Porcini
- Shiitake

● LEAFY GREENS

Your leafy greens of choice form the base of the bowl food, packed with anti-ageing, energy-fuelling antioxidants, vitamins, and minerals.

- East Asian greens (including bok choy/pak choi, tatsoi)
- Cavolo nero
- Collard greens
- Dandelion leaves
- Kale
- Lamb's lettuce
- Micro greens
- Mustard greens
- Pea shoots
- Purple sprouting broccoli
- Rainbow chard
- Rocket (arugula)
- Romaine
- Savoy cabbage
- Spinach
- Spring greens
- Swiss chard
- Turnip tops
- Watercress
- Wild garlic leaves

Complex carbohydrates provide the bulk of the energy we need. Being 'complex' means that the carbohydrates release their energy gradually, unlike sugars that cause a sudden spike, quickly followed by a low – the 'afternoon slump' most of us have experienced al one time or another. These starchy carbohydrates often contain plenty of fibre, essential for our all-important gut health. They also tend to be less energy dense than other foods, such as fats, in that they contain fewer calories for the volume of food, so they are perfect for adding to any bowl.

- Barley
- Beans (contains both protein and carbohydrate)
- Brown rice
- Buckwheat
- Bulgur
- Corn
- Couscous
- Farro
- Fermented rice
- Freekeh
- Fregola
- Jasmine rice

- Millet
- Noodles (choose either buckwheat or rice noodles)
- Oats
- Peas
- Polenta (cornmeal)
- Quinoa (contains both protein and carbohydrate)
- Red rice
- Rye
- Spelt (pearled)
- Sticky rice
- Sweet potato
- Wheatberries

● HEALTHY FATS

Healthy fats come in the form of MUFAs, PUFAs, and Omegas. We now know that far from making us fat, these healthy fats actually reduce harmful cholesterol in the body, are anti-inflammatory, and boost our brainpower. There are lots of natural ingredients that contain healthy fats, especially avocado, nuts and seeds, olive oil, and coconut oil.

- Avocado
- Coconut oil
- Extra virgin olive oil
- Oily fish (including salmon, mackerel, and tuna)
- Olives
- Nuts (including almonds, hazelnuts, and pecans)
- Nut and seed oils
- Seeds (including flax, hemp, pumpkin, and sesame)

You might want to scatter over some seeds for a little extra nourishment and crunch, or add turmeric, lemon, or apple cider vinegar to a dressing to add bonus benefits.

TOPPINGS

- Fresh herbs
- Furikake (a Japanese seasoning of black and white sesame seeds and nori flakes)
- Kimchi (see page 107)
- Miso
- Mustard
- Nutritional yeast
- Pickles (see page 107)
- Sauerkraut
- Toasted seeds
- Tamari

DRESSINGS

- Apple cider vinegar
- Buttermilk dressing (see page 104)
- Preserved lemon dressing (see page 104)
- Tahini dressing (see page 104)
- Turmeric dressing (see page 104)

POWDERS

There are a number of concentrated natural food powders now available that you might experiment with adding to your bowls. They tend to be extremely nutrient-dense.

- Beetroot (beet)
- Cacao
- Lucuma
- Matcha
- Spirulina
- Wheatgrass

BREAKFAST BOWLS

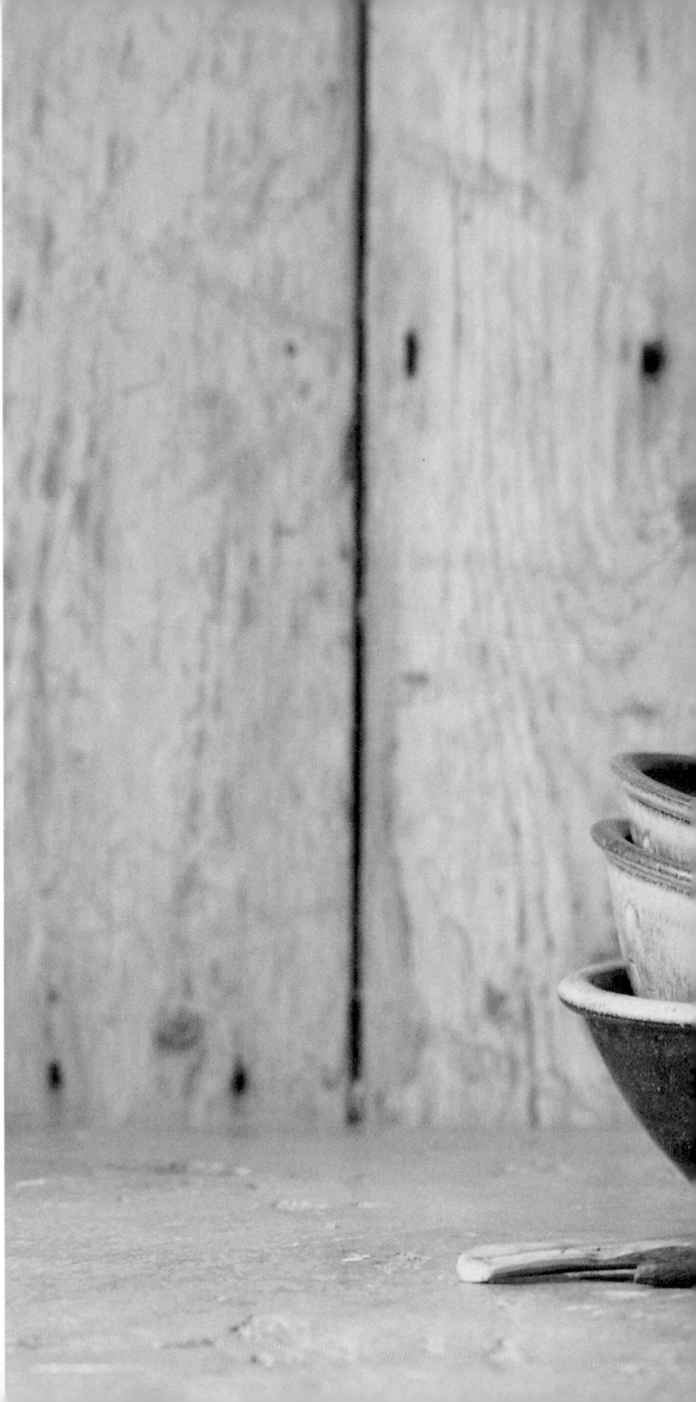

CINNAMON GRANOLA
PEAR & KALE SMOOTHIE
COCONUT YOGURT
MIXED SEEDS & DRIED BERRIES

FOR THE CINNAMON GRANOLA

Preheat the oven to 140°C/275°F/gas mark 1. Line a baking tray with baking parchment. Melt 85g (3oz/8 tbsp) coconut oil and 2 tbsp honey over a low heat. Place 100g (3½oz/1 cup) uncooked jumbo rolled oats, 20g (¾oz/2 tbsp) quinoa, 20g (¾oz/3 tbsp) pumpkin seeds, 20g (¾oz/2 tbsp) flaxseeds, 40g (1½oz/¼ cup) roughly chopped almonds, 20g (¾oz/2 tbsp) dried cranberries, and 1 tsp ground cinnamon (or more to taste) in a mixing bowl. Add the melted coconut oil and honey and stir well, until coated in the oil. Tip onto the prepared tray and spread the mixture out evenly. Bake in the oven for 50 minutes, stirring a couple of times to make sure it doesn't stick and burn. Remove from the oven and leave to cool for 10 minutes. If you want extra-crunchy granola, turn the oven off and leave the door open, with the granola still inside.

FOR THE PEAR & KALE SMOOTHIE

Blend together 1 pear, quartered and cored, a large handful of kale, tough stalks removed and leaves shredded, some coconut water and, if you need a little more sweetness, 1 tsp runny honey. (If your blender isn't powerful enough for raw kale, steam for a few minutes first.)

TO ASSEMBLE YOUR BOWL

Add the pear and kale smoothie to the bowl, then add 3 heaped tablespoonfuls of granola. Top with a spoonful of dairy-free coconut yogurt or natural (plain) yogurt, pumpkin seeds, shelled hemp seeds, and dried cranberries.

POACHED EGG
MISO ONION OAT GROATS
SPINACH
SESAME SEEDS
MIXED CRESS LEAVES

FOR THE MISO OAT GROATS AND SPINACH

Soak 55g (2oz/½ cup) oat groats in cold water overnight, then rinse and drain thoroughly. Heat 1 tsp olive oil in a saucepan and gently fry 1 chopped small onion or shallot for a few minutes, before stirring through the drained oat groats. Mix 1 tsp white or brown miso paste with a little just-boiled water to loosen, before adding about 300ml (10½fl oz/1¼ cups) just-boiled water. Stir and then add to the oats. Bring to the boil, lower the heat and simmer gently until the oats are cooked (oat groats keep a bite to them), about 15 minutes. Stir through 2 large handfuls of spinach.

FOR THE POACHED EGG

Bring a saucepan of water to a bare simmer, crack an egg into a cup then slide it into the water. Poach for 3–4 minutes, depending on how soft you like your egg, then remove with a slotted spoon.

TO ASSEMBLE YOUR BOWL

Spoon the miso onion oat groats into the bowl and top with the poached egg. Scatter over some black or white sesame seeds and a small handful of mixed cress leaves.

BERRY & SPINACH SMOOTHIE
SEASONAL FRUITS
SPINACH
PECAN GRANOLA
MIXED SEEDS
BEE POLLEN

FOR THE PECAN GRANOLA

Preheat the oven to 140°C/275°F/gas mark 1. Line a baking tray with baking parchment. Mix 1 tsp vanilla extract with 85g (3oz/8 tbsp) melted coconut oil. Place 100g (3½oz/1 cup) uncooked jumbo rolled oats, 1 tsp ground ginger, 55g (2oz/½ cup) pecan halves, 55g (2oz/½ cup) dried cranberries, 40g (1½oz/¼ cup) roughly chopped hazelnuts, and 30g (1oz/¼ cup) pumpkin seeds in a mixing bowl. Add the melted coconut oil and stir well, until coated in the oil. Tip onto the prepared tray and spread the mixture out evenly. Bake in the oven for 50 minutes, stirring a couple of times to make sure it doesn't stick and burn. Remove from the oven and leave to cool for 10 minutes. If you want extra-crunchy granola, turn the oven off and leave the door open, with the granola still inside.

FOR THE BERRY & SPINACH SMOOTHIE

Blend together 1 tbsp açaí berry powder, 1 tsp lucuma powder, ½ frozen sliced banana, a handful of blueberries, 1 tbsp almond butter, a large handful of spinach, and some almond milk.

TO ASSEMBLE YOUR BOWL

Add the berry & spinach smoothie to the bowl, then top with 3 heaped tablespoonfuls of granola. Top with fresh seasonal fruit, such as sliced figs, strawberries, redcurrants, raspberries, and blueberries, then sprinkle over a mix of flax, sesame, chia, and hemp seeds, with some bee pollen.

- **SCRAMBLED EGGS**
- **RADICCHIO**
- **COCONUT KALE**
- **SODA BREAD**
- **AVOCADO**
- **SESAME SEEDS**

FOR THE SODA BREAD

(If baking your own) Preheat the oven to 200°C/400°F/gas mark 6.
Sift 255g (9oz/1¾ cups) spelt or kamut flour, 1 tsp bicarbonate of soda
(baking soda), and ½ tsp sea salt into a large bowl, and mix. Form a well
in the middle and gradually pour in 300ml (10½fl oz/1¼ cups) natural
(plain) yogurt while stirring. You are looking for a soft dough, just beyond
sticky. On a lightly floured surface, knead the dough lightly for just a
minute to make a loose ball. (It won't feel springy because there is no
yeast.) Be quick so that the bicarbonate of soda is working as you put the
bread in the oven, and don't worry about any cracks, as they will make
the bread lovely and crusty. Place the dough on a floured baking tray and
dust generously with flour. Cut a deep cross in the top then bake for about
30 minutes. Check the loaf sounds hollow when tapped on the base, and
if it doesn't, continue to bake and check again. Remove from the oven
when ready and allow to cool.

FOR THE COCONUT KALE

Remove the woody stalks from a large handful of kale, then roughly chop
the leaves and rinse well. Heat a little coconut oil in a wok or sauté pan
and add the kale; the residual water will help to soften the kale as it cooks,
which should take about 5 minutes, stirring occasionally.

FOR THE SCRAMBLED EGGS

Whisk 2 eggs in a small bowl, then heat a non-stick pan, melt a little butter
in the pan, and add the eggs. Keep stirring over a low heat until you have
soft scrambled eggs. Season to taste.

TO ASSEMBLE YOUR BOWL

Add the kale and scrambled eggs to the bowl, with 1 sliced avocado
alongside. Sprinkle with sesame or hemp seeds, add a large handful
of radicchio leaves, then serve with a slice of toasted soda bread.

BANANA, CUCUMBER, AVOCADO, & MINT SMOOTHIE
QUINOA FLAKES
BLACK GRAPES

FOR THE BANANA, CUCUMBER, AVOCADO, & MINT SMOOTHIE

Place 2 tbsp quinoa flakes in a bowl with enough water to cover, and leave to soak for 30 minutes. Blend together ½ frozen sliced banana, ¼ cucumber, chopped, 1 small peeled, de-stoned avocado, a small handful of mint leaves, roughly chopped, the soaked quinoa flakes, and 150ml (5fl oz/⅔ cup) coconut water.

TO ASSEMBLE YOUR BOWL

Add the smoothie to the bowl and top with a small handful of halved black grapes (or blueberries) and sprinkle over a few extra quinoa flakes.

● CODDLED EGG
● BABY CAULIFLOWER
● BABY KALE
● ● ● FREGOLA SHAKSHUKA

FOR THE CAULIFLOWER

Preheat the oven to 230°C/450°F/gas mark 8. Toss 2 baby cauliflowers in a little olive oil and salt, add to a roasting tin or dish and roast in the oven for 20–25 minutes, until golden brown.

FOR THE SHAKSHUKA

Heat 2 tbsp olive oil in a heavy-based shallow pan. Add ½ chopped red onion and sauté for about 8 minutes before creating a space in the pan and adding ¼ tsp ground cumin, ¼ tsp ground coriander, ¼ tsp ground turmeric, ½ tsp paprika, ½ tsp fennel seeds, and a pinch of chilli flakes. After 30 seconds or so, stir the spices through the onion and add 1 sliced red bell pepper, 100g (3½oz/about 8–9) vine cherry tomatoes, ½ tbsp tomato paste, and ½ tsp coconut sugar. Stir, bring to a simmer, and cook for about 30 minutes.

FOR THE FREGOLA

Cook 50g (2oz/¼ cup) fregola according to the instructions on the packet, drain, and add to the shakshuka.

FOR THE CODDLED EGG

Make a hollow in the shakshuka and fregola mixture and crack an egg into it. Return to a simmer and cover with a lid for about 5 minutes, until the egg is cooked with the yolk still runny.

TO ASSEMBLE YOUR BOWL

Add the roast cauliflower to the pan and scatter over a generous handful of baby kale leaves.

KEFIR, BANANA, & CACAO SMOOTHIE
ALMOND GRANOLA
POMEGRANATE SEEDS
BEETROOT CRISPS

FOR THE ALMOND GRANOLA

Preheat the oven to 140°C/275°F/gas mark 1. Line a baking tray with baking parchment. Melt 85g (3oz/8 tbsp) coconut oil in a pan. Place 100g (3½oz/1 cup) uncooked jumbo rolled oats, 1 tsp ground ginger, 1 tbsp beetroot (beet) powder, 55g (2oz/½ cup) dried blueberries, and 55g (2oz/⅓ cup) roughly chopped almonds in a mixing bowl. Add the melted coconut oil and stir well, until coated in the oil. Tip onto the prepared tray and spread the mixture out evenly. Bake in the oven for 50 minutes, stirring a couple of times to make sure it doesn't stick and burn. Remove from the oven and leave to cool for 10 minutes. If you want extra-crunchy granola, turn the oven off and leave the door open, with the granola still inside.

FOR THE BEETROOT CRISPS

Scrub and thinly slice raw beetroot (beet), ideally with a mandolin, spread the slices out in a single layer on a baking tray, and bake in the oven at 180°C/350°F/gas mark 4 for 10–15 minutes, until crisp. Stored in an airtight container, the beetroot crisps will last 2–3 days.

FOR THE KEFIR, BANANA, & CACAO SMOOTHIE

Blend ½ frozen sliced banana, 1 tbsp cacao powder, ½ tsp matcha powder (optional), a large handful of spinach, ½ peeled and roughly chopped avocado, and 100ml (3½fl oz/⅓ cup) kefir, adding a little water or coconut water if needed to obtain the right consistency.

TO ASSEMBLE YOUR BOWL

Add the smoothie to the base of the bowl. Top with 3 heaped tablespoonfuls of granola, some beetroot crisps, and a spoonful of pomegranate seeds.

SMOKED HADDOCK OMELETTE
SPINACH, HERBS, & CRESS
FARRO
YUZU HOLLANDAISE

FOR THE FARRO
Cook 30g (1oz/2 tbsp) farro according to the packet instructions and drain.

FOR THE SPINACH, MIXED HERBS, & CRESS
Chop a handful of spinach with some mixed herbs and cress.

FOR THE YUZU HOLLANDAISE
Melt 100g (3½oz/7 tbsp) unsalted butter and skim off any white solids. Keep the butter warm while you bring a pan of water to a simmer. Place a heatproof bowl over the simmering water pan, and in the bowl whisk together 2 egg yolks and 1 tsp white wine vinegar until you have any airy foam (sabayon). Remove the bowl from the pan and whisk in a little of the melted butter, then replace the bowl over the pan and whisk constantly. Repeat until all the butter has been whisked in and the consistency is similar to mayonnaise. Add a little yuzu (or lemon juice), salt and freshly ground black pepper to taste.

FOR THE SMOKED HADDOCK
Bring a small pan of milk seasoned with a little sea salt to a simmer, add 140g (5oz) un-dyed smoked haddock fillet, and poach for 6–8 minutes until soft and flaking. Remove from the heat.

FOR THE OMELETTE
Gently beat 2 large eggs using a fork. Heat a medium frying pan (skillet) until really hot, adding 1 tsp olive oil. Add the beaten eggs and leave for about 5 seconds so that the mixture begins to bubble up, then start to pull the cooked edges into the centre and tip the runny middle to the edges. When the surface is still a little runny, fold over the omelette and remove from the heat.

TO ASSEMBLE YOUR BOWL
Serve the omelette on a bed of yuzu hollandaise, filled with the drained poached haddock, flaked into pieces, the farro, spinach, herbs, and cress.

FOR THE PUMPKIN SPICED OATS

Put 55g (2oz/½ cup) rolled oats, 100ml (3½fl oz/⅓ cup) almond milk, and 100ml (3½fl oz/¼ cup) water in a pan and bring to the boil. Reduce to a simmer and stir in 1 tbsp pumpkin purée, 1 tbsp maple syrup or runny honey, ¼ tsp ground cinnamon, and a generous pinch of ground cloves. Simmer gently for about 10 minutes, stirring every now and then. Let stand for a couple for minutes with the lid on.

FOR THE GREEN PROTEIN SMOOTHIE

Blend ½ peeled and roughly chopped avocado, a large handful of kale, tough stalks removed and leaves shredded (or use spinach), ⅓ cucumber, roughly chopped, 2 tbsp shelled hemp seeds, and as much apple juice as you need to achieve the right consistency.

TO ASSEMBLE YOUR BOWL

Spoon the spiced oats into the bowl and add a sprinkling of mixed seeds, dried cranberries, and goji berries. Serve the green protein smoothie on the side for the ultimate power breakfast.

- **SPICED FRUIT & FETA SALAD**
- **WATERMELON GAZPACHO**
- **BABY CHARD LEAVES**
- **QUINOA FLAKES**
- **EXTRA VIRGIN OLIVE OIL**
- **TOASTED QUINOA FLAKES**

FOR THE SPICED FRUIT & FETA SALAD

Preheat the oven to 200°C/400°F/gas mark 6. Chop ¼ papaya and ¼ small watermelon into cubes. Mix in a bowl with 1 tsp Chinese five-spice and ½ tsp nigella seeds, then spread out on a non-stick baking tray and roast for 10 minutes. Set aside to cool to room temperature, then mix with a handful of fresh blueberries and 30g (1oz/¼ cup) feta, cut into small cubes.

FOR THE WATERMELON GAZPACHO

Place 2 tbsp quinoa flakes in a bowl with enough water to cover, and leave to soak for 30 minutes. Blend together 200g (7oz/1 cup) chopped watermelon flesh, 90ml (3fl oz/6 tbsp) passata (strained tomatoes), the soaked quinoa flakes, a dash each of Tabasco and Worcestershire sauce, and a little extra virgin olive oil. Season to taste with sea salt and freshly ground black pepper.

TO ASSEMBLE YOUR BOWL

Cover the base of the bowl with toasted quinoa flakes. Add the gazpacho and a large handful of baby chard leaves or amaranth. Top with the roasted fruit and feta salad. Drizzle over some extra virgin olive oil.

LIGHT BOWLS

CHICKPEAS
CUCUMBER & APPLE
MIXED SALAD LEAVES
FREGOLA
HONEY MUSTARD DRESSING

FOR THE CHICKPEAS, CUCUMBER, & MIXED SALAD LEAVES
Chop ½ cucumber into batons, put into a large mixing bowl with
2 large handfuls of mixed salad leaves, and 100g (3½oz/¾ cup)
cooked chickpeas (garbanzo beans).

FOR THE FREGOLA
(Or use buckwheat for a gluten-free alternative.) Cook 40g (1½oz/¼ cup)
fregola according to the instructions on the packet. Drain, leave to cool,
then add to the mixing bowl.

FOR THE HONEY MUSTARD DRESSING
Mix together ½ tsp freshly grated or ground turmeric, 2 tsp pickled
mustard seeds and the pickling liquid (see page 107), 1 tsp runny honey,
and 3 tbsp extra virgin olive oil. Pour a little of the dressing over the salad
and mix everything gently together.

TO ASSEMBLE YOUR BOWL
Spoon the dressed salad into the bowl and top with 1 finely sliced apple.
Serve the remaining dressing alongside, adding extra to taste.

- **FRIED EGG**
- **GINGER CARROT &**
- **PICKLED CUCUMBER**
- **WATERCRESS**
- **PUY LENTILS**
- **PRESERVED LEMON YOGURT**
- **FRESH MINT**

FOR THE PICKLED CUCUMBER

Thinly slice 1 cucumber and place in a heatproof bowl. Pour 235ml (8fl oz/1 cup) apple cider vinegar and 400ml (14fl oz/1¾ cups) water into a pan, then add 3 cracked cardamom pods and ½ tbsp sea salt. Add 1 tbsp coconut sugar for sweetness, if you like. Bring to the boil and simmer for 3–4 minutes before pouring over the cucumber. Cool to room temperature and refrigerate in an airtight jar (it keeps for up to 1 month).

FOR THE PUY LENTILS

Heat a little olive oil in a pan and soften ½ small chopped onion, then add 55g (2oz/¼ cup) Puy lentils, stirring for a minute before adding plenty of hot vegetable stock (to cover generously). Simmer for about 30 minutes until cooked but still with a little bite, then drain.

FOR THE GINGER CARROT

Scrub 1 carrot, grate or julienne it, and mix with ½ tsp grated fresh ginger and a squeeze of lemon juice.

FOR THE PRESERVED LEMON YOGURT

Add ½ tsp finely chopped preserved lemon to 1 heaped tbsp natural (plain) yogurt and stir through.

FOR THE FRIED EGG

Heat a little olive oil or coconut oil in a frying pan (skillet) and fry 1 egg.

TO ASSEMBLE YOUR BOWL

Add the lentils to the bowl, then a few slices of pickled cucumber, the ginger carrot, and the fried egg. Add some watercress and chopped fresh mint, and serve with the lemon yogurt.

SESAME TOFU
GREEN BEANS
MIXED CRESS
BUCKWHEAT NOODLES
TAHINI DRESSING

FOR THE TAHINI DRESSING
Mix together the juice of 1 lime, 1 tsp coconut sugar, 1 finely chopped garlic clove, 1 tbsp fish sauce, 1 heaped tbsp tahini, 1 tsp almond butter, and 1 tsp chilli oil, adding water as needed to give the desired consistency.

FOR THE SESAME TOFU
Toss 120g (4oz/1 cup) cubed firm tofu (beancurd) in 2 tbsp sesame seeds.

FOR THE BUCKWHEAT NOODLES
Cook 85g (3oz) buckwheat noodles for 5 minutes, or according to the instructions on the packet, then drain, and rinse in cold water.

FOR THE GREEN BEANS
Steam 100g (3½oz) fresh green beans until cooked but still with a nice bite, drain, and refresh in cold water. Heat 1 tsp coconut oil in a wok or pan and add the beans to heat through.

TO ASSEMBLE YOUR BOWL
Place the tofu, noodles, and beans in your bowl, and add some mixed cress. Serve with the tahini dressing, stirring everything together in the bowl.

RAW TOMATO SAUCE
SPINACH & BASIL LEAVES
RICE & QUINOA SPAGHETTI
PRESERVED LEMON DRESSING

FOR THE ZA'ATAR SOYBEANS
Soak 55g (2oz/⅓ cup) dried soybeans overnight, then drain, rinse, and pat dry. Mix with a little olive oil and 1 tsp za'atar. Sauté in a frying pan (skillet) until golden. Add to a mixing bowl.

FOR THE RAW TOMATO SAUCE
Roughly chop 8–10 heritage cherry tomatoes and add to the soybeans in the mixing bowl, along with a generous splash of canned coconut milk.

FOR THE SPINACH & BASIL
Roughly chop a large handful each of baby spinach and basil, and add to the mixing bowl.

FOR THE RICE & QUINOA SPAGHETTI
Cook 85g (3oz) rice and quinoa spaghetti according to the instructions on the packet, then add to the mixing bowl and mix everything together.

FOR THE PRESERVED LEMON DRESSING
Mix together the finely chopped rind of 1 preserved lemon, 1 finely chopped shallot, ½ tsp coconut sugar, and a good pinch of sea salt. Add 1 part white wine vinegar to 3 parts extra virgin olive oil, to make a thick dressing.

TO ASSEMBLE YOUR BOWL
Add the soybean, spaghetti, and salad mixture to the bowl and drizzle over some preserved lemon dressing.

- CHOPPED EGG
- ASPARAGUS & SAMPHIRE
- BABY SPINACH
- BLACK QUINOA
- MUSTARD OLIVE OIL DRESSING
- RADISHES

FOR THE BLACK QUINOA
Cook 40g (1½oz/¼ cup) black quinoa in plenty of water for 20 minutes, then drain and return to the pan. Cover with a dish towel and the lid, and leave to sit for 10 minutes. Add to a mixing bowl.

FOR THE ASPARAGUS & SAMPHIRE
Snap off the woody ends of a handful of asparagus spears (about 100g/3½oz), chop into 5cm (2 in.) lengths and cut any that are thick in half lengthways. Rinse a good handful of samphire. Blanch the asparagus for 30 seconds in a pan of boiling water, then drain. Heat a wok or pan and add a little butter. Once hot, add the drained asparagus and cook for a couple of minutes before adding the samphire. Cook for a couple of minutes more, then tip into the mixing bowl.

FOR THE CHOPPED EGG & SPINACH
Add an egg in its shell to a pan of boiling water and simmer for 9 minutes. Cool under running water, then peel, chop, and add to the mixing bowl with a large handful of shredded baby spinach.

FOR THE RADISHES
Finely slice a handful of mixed radishes and add to the mixing bowl.

FOR THE MUSTARD OLIVE OIL DRESSING
Mix together 1 tsp Dijon mustard and 2 tbsp lime juice or balsamic vinegar, 6 tbsp extra virgin olive oil, and plenty of seasoning. Add 2 tbsp to the ingredients in the mixing bowl and mix through, adding more if needed.

TO ASSEMBLE YOUR BOWL
Add the dressed salad to the bowl.

● **SALT & PEPPER TOFU**

● **BRUSSELS SPROUTS & BROCCOLI**

● **SPROUT FLOWERS**

● **BULGUR WHEAT**

● **LIME & SESAME DRESSING**

FOR THE BRUSSELS SPROUTS & BROCCOLI

Finely slice a handful of raw Brussels sprouts, using a mandolin or very sharp knife. Cut a third of a broccoli head into small florets. (You can steam the broccoli for a few minutes then refresh in iced water if you struggle to eat raw green vegetables.)

FOR THE SPROUT FLOWERS

Rinse and sauté in a little coconut oil.

FOR THE SALT & PEPPER TOFU

Slice 100g (3½oz/¾ cup) firm tofu (beancurd) into rectangular slabs. Crush 1 tsp mixed peppercorns (black, pink, green, and Sichuan) in a pestle and mortar and mix with ½ tsp flaky sea salt and 3 tsp cornflour (cornstarch). Coat the tofu slices in the seasoned flour and shallow-fry in a pan with very hot groundnut (peanut) oil.

FOR THE BULGUR WHEAT

Simmer 55g (2oz/¼ cup) bulgur wheat in water with 1 tsp vegetable bouillon (powder) until cooked. Drain.

FOR THE LIME & SESAME DRESSING

Mix together 3 tbsp toasted sesame oil, 1 tsp sesame seeds, the juice of 1 lime, a splash of fish sauce, and 1 tsp coconut sugar.

TO ASSEMBLE YOUR BOWL

Cover the base of the bowl with bulgur wheat, then add the sprout flowers or kale. Toss the vegetables in some of the dressing and add to the bowl, then top with the salt and pepper tofu, and serve with more dressing.

● **RED LENTIL HUMMUS**
● **RED BELL & CHILLI PEPPERS**
● **WATERCRESS**
● **CAMOMILE BAKED SWEET POTATO**
● **OLIVE OIL DRESSING**
● **YEAST FLAKES**

FOR THE CAMOMILE BAKED SWEET POTATO

Preheat the oven to 190°C/375°F/gas mark 5. Spread 1 tbsp camomile flowers (loose tea) over the base of a small roasting dish and place 1 scrubbed sweet potato in the dish. Add water to come a third of the way up the potato, cover with foil, and bake for about 45 minutes or until you can pierce the potato easily with a sharp knife. Remove from the oven and turn the oven up to 230°C/450°F/gas mark 8. Carefully halve the sweet potato lengthways and transfer to an ovenproof griddle pan or skillet. Dot a little butter on top, then drizzle over 1 tbsp runny honey. Roast in the hot oven for 10 minutes, basting halfway through. Allow the potato to cool a little before cutting into wedges.

FOR THE RED LENTIL HUMMUS

Cook 100g (3½oz/½ cup) dried red split lentils in water and drain. When cool, add to a food processor and pulse until quite smooth before adding 1 small crushed garlic clove, the juice of 1 small lemon, 1 tbsp tahini, and ¼ tsp sea salt. Blend to a soft hummus texture, adding water as needed. Taste for seasoning and to check if you have enough lemon juice.

FOR THE RED BELL & CHILLI PEPPERS

Deseed and thinly slice 1 red bell pepper and ½ red chilli pepper.

TO ASSEMBLE YOUR BOWL

Add a couple of heaped spoonfuls of the lentil hummus and arrange the sweet potato wedges on top. Scatter over the bell pepper and chilli pepper, a good handful of watercress, and some yeast flakes. Drizzle over just a little extra virgin olive oil and a pinch of flaky sea salt to serve.

- **SOFT GOAT CHEESE**
- **PEACH, ORANGE, &**
  PINK GRAPEFRUIT
- **MUSTARD LEAF & FENNEL FRONDS**
- **TOASTED QUINOA**
- **POMEGRANATE OLIVE OIL**
  DRESSING
- **POMEGRANATE SEEDS**

FOR THE TOASTED QUINOA
Soak 40g (1½oz/¼ cup) quinoa for a few minutes then tip into a sieve (strainer) and rinse through. Heat a dry saucepan and add the quinoa, toasting until the grains separate and become fragrant, then add water or stock to cover, bring to the boil, then reduce to a low simmer. Cover and cook for 15–20 minutes, then drain and return the quinoa to the pan, cover with a dish towel and the lid, and leave to sit for 10 minutes before adding to a mixing bowl.

FOR THE PEACH, ORANGE, & PINK GRAPEFRUIT
Halve and stone a peach, cut into slices. Peel and slice an orange and remove the pith. Peel and segment half of a pink grapefruit. Add these to the mixing bowl.

FOR THE MUSTARD LEAF & FENNEL FRONDS
Add a good handful of mustard (or other) leaves and fennel fronds to the mixing bowl.

FOR THE POMEGRANATE OLIVE OIL DRESSING
Mix together some extra virgin olive oil, pomegranate molasses (or honey), and sherry vinegar, to taste. Drizzle a little over the salad in the bowl and gently mix together.

TO ASSEMBLE YOUR BOWL
Place the dressed salad in the bowl. Top with some soft goat cheese and scatter over pomegranate seeds.

- ## GOAT CURD
- ## BAKED BEETROOT
- ## MIXED SALAD LEAVES
- ## SPROUTED BUCKWHEAT
- ## DILL DRESSING
- ## SWEET POTATO CRISPS

FOR THE BAKED BEETROOT

Preheat the oven to 200°C/400°F/gas mark 6. Wash a couple of medium beetroot (beets) in a mixture of colours, if you like, and trim off the stalks to about 2.5cm (1 in.). Place in a roasting tray and pour over 2 tbsp apple cider vinegar. Pour about a 2.5cm (1 in.) depth of water around the bottom of the beetroot and cover with foil, then bake in the oven for about 45–60 minutes, until you can pierce one easily with a sharp knife. Allow to cool a little before rubbing off the outer skin and cutting them into quarters.

FOR THE SWEET POTATO CRISPS

Thinly slice a sweet potato, ideally using a mandolin, spread out on a baking tray and bake in the oven at 180°C/350°F/gas mark 4 until crisp, about 10–15 minutes.

FOR THE SPROUTED BUCKWHEAT

Either buy sprouted buckwheat that is ready to eat, or rinse 40g (1½oz/ ¼ cup) roasted buckwheat and cook for 10–15 minutes in a pan of simmering water before draining.

FOR THE DILL DRESSING

Mix together 2 tbsp raspberry or white balsamic vinegar and 6 tbsp extra virgin olive oil with plenty of finely chopped dill and a little sea salt. In a large mixing bowl, mix together some salad leaves, the baked beetroot, and a couple of tablespoons of the dressing.

TO ASSEMBLE YOUR BOWL

Add the dressed beetroot and a generous handful of mixed salad leaves to the bowl, then top with some goat curd, the buckwheat, and scatter over the sweet potato crisps.

LIME RICOTTA
BABY CARROTS &
WATERMELON RADISH
LAMB'S LETTUCE & FENNEL FRONDS
PEARLED SPELT
CARROT JUICE DRESSING

FOR THE ROASTED CARROTS
Preheat the oven to 200°C/400°F/gas mark 6. Scrub 50g (2oz) baby carrots and trim the greens. Toss the carrots in a little olive oil, cumin seeds, and salt and roast in the oven for about 20 minutes, until beginning to caramelize. Sprinkle over a little white balsamic or sherry vinegar and allow to cool.

FOR THE PEARLED SPELT
Bring a pan of water to the boil, add 40g (1½oz/¼ cup) pearled spelt, and simmer for about 20 minutes until cooked, then drain.

FOR THE LIME RICOTTA
Mix the finely grated zest of ½ lime with 40g (1½oz/¼ cup) ricotta.

FOR THE LAMB'S LETTUCE & WATERMELON RADISH
Rinse a big handful of lamb's lettuce and thinly slice a watermelon radish or a few breakfast radishes.

FOR THE CARROT JUICE DRESSING
Scrub 50g (2oz) baby carrots and trim the greens. Either juice a carrot or use cold-pressed carrot juice and add a little carrot juice to the roasted and raw carrots, lamb's lettuce, watermelon radish, and pearled spelt, then gently toss together.

TO ASSEMBLE YOUR BOWL
Put the tossed ingredients into the bowl and add a couple of spoonfuls of the lime ricotta, a few fennel fronds, and sea salt to taste.

PERSIAN CHICKEN SKEWERS
GYPSY SALAD
RED RICE
TAMARIND YOGURT

FOR THE PERSIAN CHICKEN SKEWERS

Marinate 1 large or 2 small boneless, skinless chicken thighs in a mixture of ground ginger, allspice, ground turmeric and ground cumin, crushed garlic, a little olive oil, and some lemon juice, ideally overnight in the refrigerator. Cut the marinated thighs into smaller pieces and thread onto skewers before grilling (broiling) for a few minutes on each side until cooked through.

FOR THE RED RICE

Cook 55g (2oz/¼ cup) red rice according to the instructions on the packet.

FOR THE GYPSY SALAD

Mix together grated carrot and fennel, with some chopped fennel fronds, chopped dried apricots, and toasted flaked (slivered) almonds. Add a little sea salt.

FOR THE TAMARIND YOGURT

Mix 1 tsp tamarind paste (loosened in a little hot water if very thick) into some natural (plain) yogurt. Toss the salad in a little of the tamarind yogurt.

TO ASSEMBLE YOUR BOWL

Add the rice and salad to the bowl, top with the chicken, and serve with the rest of the tamarind yogurt.

- **MACKEREL FILLET**
- **CUCUMBER & MELON SALAD**
- **LAMB'S LETTUCE & MIXED HERBS**
- **SUSHI RICE**
- **OLIVE OIL DRESSING**
- **SPELT FLATBREAD**

FOR THE SUSHI RICE

Cook 55g (2oz/¼ cup) sushi or Thai sticky rice according to the instructions on the packet, leaving the lid on for 10 minutes after cooking to continue to steam. Stir through some chopped spring onion (scallion) and furikake or sesame seeds.

FOR THE HERB, CUCUMBER & MELON SALAD

If you can find cucamelons, which have a flavour of melon and cucumber, slice a handful lengthways. (If you can't find cucamelons, use honeydew or galia melon.) Mix with ½ chopped cucumber, 1 finely chopped shallot, chopped fresh coriander (cilantro), mint and parsley, and some toasted coriander seeds. Mix with a little extra virgin olive oil and season with sea salt and freshly ground black pepper.

FOR THE SPELT FLATBREAD

To make 4 flatbreads, mix 125g (4½oz/1 level cup) wholemeal (wholewheat) spelt flour with a good pinch of sea salt. Add 120ml (4fl oz/½ cup) water a little at a time, kneading until it forms a soft dough. Sprinkle a little more flour over your work surface and divide the dough in four, rolling into balls. Squash a ball onto the floured surface and roll into a thin disc. Heat a large dry frying pan (skillet) and, once hot, place a flatbread in the pan and cook for a minute or so until it begins to bubble, then flip over and cook the other side until golden. Repeat with the remaining dough.

FOR THE MACKEREL

Heat a little olive oil in a frying pan. Pat a mackerel fillet dry and season the flesh before placing skin-side down in the hot pan. Cook for 1–2 minutes before flipping over and taking off the heat to finish cooking.

TO ASSEMBLE YOUR BOWL

Add a flatbread and top with the mackerel and rice. Add some cucumber salad to the side and top with sprigs of lamb's lettuce.

SALMON TARTARE
CUCUMBER
SPINACH
FARRO
WASABI MAYONNAISE
FRESH HERBS

FOR THE SPINACH & FARRO

Bring a pan of water to the boil, add ½ tsp sea salt, and 55g (2oz/¼ cup) farro, reduce the heat and simmer for 30 minutes or until cooked. Drain. Shred a handful of spinach and mix through the cooked farro.

FOR THE WASABI MAYONNAISE

Whisk together 1 egg yolk, ¼ tsp wasabi, ½ tsp sea salt, and 1 tbsp brown rice vinegar or sushi-su, then add 150ml (5fl oz/⅔ cup) olive oil drop by drop as you whisk vigorously to emulsify. Alternatively, mix a little wasabi into Greek yogurt.

FOR THE SALMON TARTARE

Cut a 100g (3½oz) sushi-grade salmon fillet, from a quality fishmonger, into small, neat cubes.

FOR THE CUCUMBER

Peel about 5 long, thin ribbons of cucumber using a swivel vegetable peeler, then cut about a third of the remaining cucumber into small cubes. Mix the cubed cucumber and the cubed salmon into the farro and spinach. Squeeze over some lemon or lime juice and mix in some of the wasabi mayonnaise.

TO ASSEMBLE YOUR BOWL

Brush some more of the wasabi mayonnaise around the rim of the bowl and stick the cucumber ribbons around the edge. Fill the bowl with the salmon tartare, cucumber, and spinach and farro mixture, then garnish with marigold leaves or any fresh herb.

- **SALMON SASHIMI**
- **SEA VEGETABLE SALAD**
- **EAST ASIAN GREENS**
- **STICKY RICE**
- **TAMARI DRESSING**
- **FURIKAKE**

FOR THE STICKY RICE

Cook 55g (2oz/¼ cup) sushi or Thai sticky rice according to the instructions on the packet, keeping the lid on and, once cooked, leaving the lid on for 10 minutes to continue to steam before mixing with a rice paddle or spatula.

FOR THE SALMON SASHIMI

Slice 100g (3½oz) raw sushi-grade salmon into 5mm (¼ in.) slices.

FOR THE SEA VEGETABLE SALAD

Soak 5g (¼oz) dried sea vegetable salad in water for a few minutes.

FOR THE EAST ASIAN GREENS

If you can find tatsoi, these are good raw, or soften bok choy in a hot wok with a little sesame oil until just wilted.

FOR THE TAMARI DRESSING

Mix together 2 tbsp tamari (wheat-free soy sauce), ½ tsp grated fresh ginger, 1 tbsp brown rice vinegar, and 1 tbsp lime juice.

TO ASSEMBLE YOUR BOWL

Add the sticky rice, salmon sashimi, sea vegetable salad and tatsoi or bok choy to your bowl and top with a few beansprouts, thin slices of red onion, some pickled ginger, and a pea-sized dab of wasabi. Scatter over furikake or sesame seeds. Serve the tamari dressing as a dipping sauce.

CRAYFISH RICE VERMICELLI
GRAPEFRUIT & MINT SALSA
GINGER KALE & FENNEL FRONDS
AVOCADO

FOR THE GRAPEFRUIT & MINT SALSA

Peel, segment and chop a pink grapefruit. Mix with some sweet chilli sauce or 1 tsp freshly chopped chilli pepper and 2 tbsp honey, 2 tbsp red wine vinegar, and plenty of freshly chopped mint leaves.

FOR THE CRAYFISH RICE VERMICELLI

Mix 80–100g (3½oz/½ cup) cooked and cooled crayfish (large shrimp) with 55g (2oz/¾ cup) cooked and cooled rice vermicelli.

FOR THE GINGER KALE & FENNEL FRONDS

Rinse a large handful of kale, remove the thick stalks, shred, and sauté in a little coconut oil and chopped ginger. Allow to cool then season with sea salt and toss gently with the crayfish and rice vermicelli. Add some thinly sliced raw fennel, including the fronds, and ½ diced avocado, and check again for seasoning.

TO ASSEMBLE YOUR BOWL

Add the crayfish and rice vermicelli salad to the bowl and serve with a few tablespoonfuls of the grapefruit and mint salsa.

GARLIC MUSSELS
SEA SPAGHETTI
SALTY FINGERS
RED RICE

FOR THE SEA SPAGHETTI

Soak 15g (½oz) sea spaghetti in cold water for 30 minutes. Bring a pan of water to the boil, add the drained sea spaghetti and boil until tender. Drain and toss in a little melted coconut oil.

FOR THE RED RICE

Rinse 55g (2oz/¼ cup) red rice and add to a pan of boiling water. Reduce to a simmer and cook for 30–40 minutes, or until tender. Drain.

FOR THE GARLIC MUSSELS

Check through 500g (18oz/about 15–20) mussels, discarding any open ones that do not close when tapped firmly. Scrub off any barnacles. Heat 1 tbsp olive oil in a heavy-based pan, add ¼ finely chopped onion and 1 finely chopped garlic clove, and cook gently until soft. Pour in 50ml (1⅔fl oz/3½ tbsp) white wine, then tip in the mussels. Give them a good stir, cover, then remove from the heat. They will continue to cook and open in the residual heat.

TO ASSEMBLE YOUR BOWL

Pick the freshly cooked mussels from their shells and put in the bowl, pouring over the broth from the pan. Add the red rice, sea spaghetti, and some salty fingers (a type of coastal plant vegetable) or watercress.

MARINATED FETA
ROAST TOMATOES
CAVOLO NERO
SPICED BEANS
LAND CRESS

FOR THE MARINATED FETA

Gently fry ¼ tsp each of black onion and coriander seeds in 1½ tbsp olive oil to release the aromas. Add these to 55g (2oz/½ cup) cubed feta, along with the frying oil, and stir well. Marinate in the refrigerator, overnight if possible.

FOR THE ROAST TOMATOES

Preheat the oven to 200°C/400°F/gas mark 6. Put a string of cherry tomatoes on the vine onto a roasting tray and roast in the oven until just bursting, about 15 minutes.

FOR THE SPICED BEANS

Heat 1 tbsp olive oil in a pan with ½ tsp finely grated lemon zest, add 1 chopped spring onion (scallion) and cook until softened. Add 55g (2oz/½ cup) canned, rinsed chickpeas (garbanzo beans) and 40g (1½oz/¼ cup) canned, rinsed borlotti beans along with ¼ tsp ground cumin and a pinch of chilli flakes. Warm through and taste for seasoning.

FOR THE CAVOLO NERO

Remove the woody stalks from a handful of cavolo nero leaves, shred the leaves, and massage in some apple cider vinegar to soften.

TO ASSEMBLE YOUR BOWL

Add the spiced beans, cavolo nero, and roast tomatoes to your bowl, crumble in the feta, scatter over some cress, and finish with a squeeze of lemon juice.

- **GRIDDLED HALLOUMI**
- **ROAST JERUSALEM ARTICHOKES**
- **BURST TOMATOES & ASPARAGUS**
- **JASMINE RICE**
- **HONEY LEMON DRESSING**
- **PICKLED RED ONION**

FOR THE ROAST JERUSALEM ARTICHOKES & BURST TOMATOES
Preheat the oven to 220°C/425°F/gas mark 7. Wash 3 or 4 Jerusalem
artichokes, sprinkle with a little sea salt, and roast whole for about
20 minutes, or until they can be easily pierced with a sharp knife. Turn
off the oven. Mix a handful of datterini or cherry tomatoes in a little olive
oil and place on a roasting tray in the oven after you have removed the
artichokes. These will warm and slightly burst in the residual heat.

FOR THE JASMINE RICE
Measure 40g (1½oz/¼ cup) long-grain jasmine rice, rinse well, and add to
a pan with 1.5 times its volume of water. Bring to the boil then reduce the
heat and simmer for 15–20 minutes, uncovered, until cooked. Drain then
return to the pan, cover with a dish towel and the lid, and leave to sit for
a few minutes.

FOR THE ASPARAGUS
Griddle 4–6 asparagus spears, with the woody ends snapped off, in a hot
pan, until coloured and cooked, but still with a nice bite.

FOR THE GRIDDLED HALLOUMI
Griddle 3 slices of halloumi in a hot pan, for about 4 minutes on each
side, turning every now and then, until golden on the outside and soft
in the middle.

FOR THE HONEY LEMON DRESSING
Mix together some lemon juice, a little honey, and some extra virgin
olive oil.

TO ASSEMBLE YOUR BOWL
Arrange the jasmine rice, Jerusalem artichokes, tomatoes, asparagus,
and halloumi in your bowl, adding some pickled red onion (see page 107).
Drizzle over the dressing.

POMEGRANATE LABNEH
BABY LEEKS
BABY SPINACH
MUJADARA LENTILS & RICE
PISTACHIOS
POMEGRANATE SEEDS

FOR THE POMEGRANATE LABNEH

Strain some natural (plain) yogurt through a muslin cloth into a bowl overnight in the refrigerator, to leave a thick yogurt (you can use the whey liquid left over for tenderizing meat or adding to smoothies). Add a little pomegranate molasses to the strained yogurt, spoon into a small dish, and sprinkle with some pomegranate seeds and chopped pistachios.

FOR THE MUJADARA LENTILS & RICE

Add 55g (2oz/¼ cup) Puy lentils, ½ peeled small onion, and 1 tsp vegetable bouillon powder to a pan of water, bring to the boil then reduce to a simmer for about 25 minutes, or until the lentils are cooked and still have a little bite, then drain. In a separate pan, cook 55g (2oz/⅓ cup) long-grain rice according to the instructions on the packet.

FOR THE BABY LEEKS & BABY SPINACH

Heat a little coconut oil or butter in a griddle pan and griddle 3 baby leeks until soft and lightly charred, about 7–10 minutes (or sauté 1 regular leek, sliced, in a pan). Mix the leeks with the lentils, a handful of shredded baby spinach, some pomegranate seeds, and chopped pistachios.

TO ASSEMBLE YOUR BOWL

Add some rice first, then top with the lentil mixture. Enjoy with pomegranate labneh on the side.

VEGETABLE TAGINE
SWISS CHARD
WHOLEWHEAT COUSCOUS
YOGURT
ROSEWATER

FOR THE VEGETABLE TAGINE

(Enough for 4 servings) Preheat the oven to 175°C/350°F/gas mark 4. Scrub 1 carrot and cut into chunks. Peel ¼ butternut squash and ¼ medium celeriac (celery root) and cut into roughly 2.5cm (1 in.) dice. Cut 1 small turnip, 1 parsnip, 1 aubergine (eggplant), and 1 medium courgette (zucchini) into roughly 2.5cm (1 in.) dice. Combine the following with 100ml (3⅓fl oz/⅓ cup) olive oil: 1 tbsp sweet paprika, ½ tbsp ground ginger, ½ tbsp chilli flakes, ½ tbsp ground cumin, ½ tbsp ground coriander, the seeds of 4 cardamom pods, 1 crushed garlic clove, the juice of 1 lemon, ½ tsp flaky sea salt and some black pepper. Mix the spiced oil with all the vegetables except the courgette, making sure they are coated well. Heat a large flameproof casserole, add the spiced vegetables, and sauté for a few minutes. Add a 425g (15oz) can of drained chickpeas (garbanzo beans), 250ml (8½fl oz/1 cup) vegetable stock, and 1 tbsp tomato paste. Give a stir, cover, and put in the oven for about 10 minutes, then add the courgette and cook for another 20–30 minutes, until the vegetables are cooked and the flavours have all infused.

FOR THE COUSCOUS

Put 55g (2oz/⅓ cup) wholewheat couscous per serving into a heatproof bowl. Pour over just-boiled water so the grains are just covered and add a drizzle of extra virgin olive oil. Cover with a plate and, after 5 minutes, check the water has been absorbed. Fluff with a fork.

FOR THE SWISS CHARD

Roughly shred a large handful of rinsed Swiss chard per serving, and massage in a little apple cider vinegar.

TO ASSEMBLE YOUR BOWL

Spoon in some vegetable tagine, add the couscous and Swiss chard, sprinkle over a few drops of rosewater, and serve with natural (plain) yogurt.

MUSHROOM & TOFU BIBIMBAP
RAW VEGETABLES
BOK CHOY
BROWN RICE
FRIED EGG
GOCHUJANG SAUCE

FOR THE GOCHUJANG SAUCE
Mix together 1 tbsp gochujang paste, 1 tbsp rice vinegar, 1 tbsp light soy sauce, ½ tsp coconut sugar, ½ tbsp sesame oil, ½ tbsp sesame seeds, and 1 finely chopped spring onion (scallion).

FOR THE BROWN RICE
Cook 55g (2oz/¼ cup) brown rice according to the instructions on the packet (about 30 minutes), then drain.

FOR THE TOFU
Cut 85g (3oz/¾ cup) firm tofu (beancurd) into cubes and sprinkle with black sesame seeds and flaky sea salt.

FOR THE MUSHROOMS, RAW VEGETABLES, & BOK CHOY
Sauté a handful of exotic mushrooms, such as enoki, in a little sesame oil. Shave 1 carrot into ribbons using a swivel vegetable peeler, or use a spiralizer. Finely slice 1 spring onion (scallion) and separate out the leaves of 1 baby bok choy.

FOR THE FRIED EGG
Fry 1 egg in a little olive oil.

TO ASSEMBLE YOUR BOWL
Spoon the brown rice into the middle of the bowl and top with the fried egg, in the very centre so that the yolk will stay exposed. Add the tofu, mushrooms, raw vegetables, and bok choy around the sides of the yolk, and serve with the gochujang sauce and kimchi (see page 107) on the side.

- **CRUMBLED TOFU**
- **SRIRACHA TOMATO SAUCE**
- **SAUTÉED GREENS**
- **TOASTED MILLET**
- **HONEY CASHEWS**

FOR THE HONEY CASHEWS

Preheat the oven to 180°C/350°F/gas mark 4. Toss 100g (3½oz/¾ cup) raw cashews in a little groundnut (peanut) or olive oil and sea salt. Melt 3 tbsp coconut sugar with 2 tbsp honey and 1 tbsp water in a small pan over a low heat. Pour this over the nuts, mix well to coat, and spread them out on a roasting tray. Roast for about 20 minutes until golden, stirring halfway. Allow to cool before chopping a handful. Transfer the rest to an airtight jar.

FOR THE SRIRACHA TOMATO SAUCE

Place a handful of tomatoes on the vine on a roasting tray, drizzle with olive oil, and sprinkle with sea salt. Roast in the oven at 190°C/375°F/gas mark 5 until just bursting, about 12 minutes. Leave until cool enough to take off the vine, then blitz in a food processor with 1 tbsp sriracha sauce.

FOR THE TOASTED MILLET

Heat a dry saucepan and add the 50g (2oz/1/4 cup) millet to toast for a couple of minutes until the grains begin to brown. Add twice the volume of water as millet with ½ tsp vegetable bouillon powder and bring to the boil, then reduce to a simmer, cover, and cook for about 15 minutes until cooked and all the liquid has been absorbed. Remove from the heat, place a dish towel over the pan and then the lid, letting it sit for 10 minutes before fluffing with a fork.

FOR THE GREENS

Heat ½ tsp coconut oil in a wok or pan and sauté a handful each of kale, spring greens, bok choy, and savoy cabbage. Stir through the millet.

FOR THE CRUMBLED TOFU

Crumble 85g (3oz/¾ cup) firm tofu (beancurd) into the greens and millet, then mix through.

TO ASSEMBLE YOUR BOWL

Add the cooked millet, sautéed greens, and crumbled tofu mixture to the bowl, then top with the chopped honey cashews. Serve with warm sriracha tomato sauce.

GIROLLE & SHIITAKE RYE RISOTTO
BABY CHARD
WET WALNUTS
PARMESAN SHAVINGS

FOR THE RYE RISOTTO

Soak 55g (2oz/¼ cup) dried rye or spelt grains in plenty of water overnight, then rinse and drain. Sauté ½ finely chopped onion in a little butter or olive oil, add the rye grains, and stir through for 1 minute. Meanwhile, heat 300ml (10½fl oz/1¼ cups) chicken stock in a separate pan. Ladle half the stock into the rye grains and cook as you would a risotto, stirring often, and adding more stock as needed. Rye will have a nutty bite even when cooked, which will take about 1 hour.

FOR THE GIROLLE & SHIITAKE MUSHROOMS

Clean 30g (1oz) fresh girolle mushrooms and 55g (2oz) fresh shiitake mushrooms, then sauté in 1 tbsp melted unsalted butter. Season with a little sea salt and, if you like, a pinch of yeast flakes.

FOR THE BABY CHARD

Wilt a good handful of baby chard leaves in the same pan as the mushrooms were cooked in, or in a steamer.

TO ASSEMBLE YOUR BOWL

Spoon the rye risotto into the bowl and place the wilted baby chard on top. Add the mushrooms, some wet walnuts (when in season), generous shavings of Parmesan, and a few sprigs of mustard leaves.

CHILLI CHICKEN
CORN & AVOCADO SALSA
DANDELION LEAVES
BLACK QUINOA
ZESTY SOUR CREAM

FOR THE CHILLI CHICKEN
Preheat the oven to 180°C/350°F/gas mark 4. Marinate 1 boneless chicken breast (skin on) for 10 minutes in 2 tbsp natural (plain) yogurt mixed with the juice of 1 lime and a pinch of chilli flakes. Heat an ovenproof griddle pan until hot, add the chicken, and sear on both sides, then transfer to the oven for 8 minutes, until cooked through and tender.

FOR THE CORN & AVOCADO SALSA
If using fresh corn, brush the kernels of a fresh cob with melted coconut oil and griddle until lightly charred all over. When cool enough to handle, stand the cob on its end and use a sharp knife to slice the kernels down off the cob. Alternatively, melt a little coconut oil in a frying pan (skillet) and sauté 85g (3oz/½ cup) frozen kernels (from frozen). In a large bowl, mix the corn with 1 small peeled and diced avocado, ½ deseeded and finely chopped green chilli pepper, plenty of chopped coriander (cilantro), a good pinch of sea salt, and some lime juice.

FOR THE BLACK QUINOA
Cook 55g (2oz/⅓ cup) black quinoa (or any type of quinoa) according to the instructions on the packet, and stir through 1 tbsp ponzu or light soy sauce.

TO ASSEMBLE YOUR BOWL
Cut the chicken into slices and add to the bowl with the quinoa, corn, and avocado salsa, and some dandelion leaves (or any salad leaves), then top with a dollop of sour cream or natural (plain) yogurt garnished with some grated or pared lime zest.

● LEMON ROAST CHICKEN
● GRILLED ASPARAGUS
● MIXED CRESS SALAD
● BULGUR & QUINOA
● CHICKEN CREAM

FOR THE LEMON ROAST CHICKEN

Preheat the oven to 190°C/375°F/gas mark 5. Rub the skin of a small chicken (1–1.25kg/35–44oz) with a halved lemon. Place the lemon halves in the cavity. Sprinkle sea salt over the skin and smear over some softened butter, then place the chicken on a wire rack in a roasting tin. Roast for 1 hour to 1 hour 10 minutes, until the juices run clear, then cover and rest for 5–10 minutes before carving three thick slices per bowl. (The remainder of the chicken can be wrapped and kept in the refrigerator for up to 3 days. Alternatively, remove the thighs before roasting and use them to make the Chicken Fattee on page 95.)

FOR THE CHICKEN CREAM

Take some trimmings from the roast chicken and blend in a food processor with equal quantities of chicken stock and almond milk. You are looking for a thick, creamy consistency. Pass this through a sieve (strainer) for a smoother texture and taste for seasoning, adding a little sea salt and white pepper.

FOR THE GRILLED ASPARAGUS

Snap off the woody ends of 6 asparagus spears, toss in a little olive oil and grill (broil), turning as they cook.

FOR THE BULGUR & QUINOA

Bring a pan of water to the boil, add a 55g (2oz/¼ cup) mixture of bulgur and quinoa, then simmer for 12 minutes until cooked. Drain and return to the pan, cover with a dish towel and the lid, and rest for a few minutes before fluffing up with a fork.

TO ASSEMBLE YOUR BOWL

Put some slices of chicken breast in the bowl, with the bulgur and quinoa alongside. Add the asparagus, top with a handful of mixed cress, and serve with the chicken cream on the side.

- **CHICKEN FATTEE**
- **SPICED AUBERGINE**
- **COLESLAW**
- **LITTLE GEM LETTUCE**
- **SOFT SEEDED TORTILLA**
- **LIME YOGURT**

FOR THE CHICKEN FATTEE

Rub 2 chicken thighs all over with a mixture of 1 tbsp sea salt, 1 tbsp brown sugar, and 1 tsp of creole spice mix (see page 104), then leave to dry-brine in the refrigerator for 1 hour or preferably overnight. Wash off the brine mixture and pat dry. Preheat the oven to 175°C/350°F/gas mark 4. Heat a little groundnut (peanut) oil in an ovenproof frying pan (skillet) and add the thighs, skin-side down, to seal. Add 1 tsp butter to the pan and roast in the oven for 25 minutes, until cooked through. Allow to cool a little before pulling off the meat from the bone.

FOR THE SPICED AUBERGINE

Chop an aubergine (eggplant) into small cubes and toss in olive oil and ¼ tsp each of fennel seeds, mustard seeds, cumin seeds, and sea salt. Spread out on a roasting tray and roast in the oven at 220°C/425°F/ gas mark 7 for about 10 minutes.

FOR THE COLESLAW

Finely grate 1 carrot, 1 small courgette (zucchini), and ¼ green cabbage. Squeeze the grated courgette to remove any excess liquid. Toss the grated vegetables in a little apple cider vinegar and extra virgin olive oil.

FOR THE LIME YOGURT

Mix a little grated lime zest into thick natural (plain) yogurt.

TO ASSEMBLE YOUR BOWL

Line the bowl with a soft seeded tortilla and add the chicken, aubergine, coleslaw, little gem or round lettuce leaves, and a spoonful of lime yogurt. Serve with a lime wedge to squeeze over.

SEARED SIRLOIN
RAW KOHLRABI
TURNIP TOPS
JASMINE RICE
SUSHI GINGER

FOR THE JASMINE RICE
Measure 55g (2oz/⅓ cup) long-grain Jasmine rice, rinse well, and add to a saucepan with 1.5 times its volume of water. Bring to the boil, then reduce the heat to a simmer, cover, and cook for 15 minutes, until the water is absorbed. Remove from the heat and place a dish towel over the pan, replacing the lid, and allow to sit for a few minutes before fluffing the rice.

FOR THE SEARED SIRLOIN
Season a sirloin steak with sea salt and heat a ridged griddle pan. Once very hot, sear the steak for 4 minutes on each side (for medium-rare), giving it a quarter turn after 2 minutes to create criss-cross sear marks. Remove from the heat and allow to rest in the pan while you heat up the grill (broiler). Add a knob of butter to the top of the steak and flash under the hot grill for a couple of minutes before transferring to a board. Rest for a few minutes before slicing.

FOR THE TURNIP TOPS (OR ANY GREENS)
Rinse, trim, and sauté a handful of turnip tops in 1 tbsp melted coconut oil, seasoning with a little sea salt.

FOR THE RAW KOHLRABI & SUSHI GINGER
Peel a young, fresh kohlrabi, cut into small cubes and put into a small bowl. Put a little sushi ginger in a second small bowl.

TO ASSEMBLE YOUR BOWL
Spoon the rice into the bowl, place the turnip tops or greens on the rice, then the sliced steak on top. Serve with the kohlrabi and sushi ginger.

● **LAMB**
● **SPRING ONION & GREEN CHILLI**
● **PURPLE SPROUTING BROCCOLI**
● **COCONUT POLENTA**
● **TOASTED PINE NUTS**

FOR THE LAMB

Mix 85g (3oz/scant ½ cup) minced (ground) lamb with 1 tsp laksa paste (see page 107) and leave to marinate for 30 minutes. Heat a little groundnut (peanut) oil in a frying pan (skillet) and fry 3 curry leaves for a couple of minutes before adding the minced lamb. Fry until the minced lamb is browned and cooked through, then add a little stock for it to continue simmering and softening for another 10–15 minutes. Stir through some chopped coriander (cilantro).

FOR THE COCONUT POLENTA

Bring 80ml (2½fl oz/5 tbsp) coconut milk (from a carton, not a can) to the boil in a saucepan and stir in 40g (1½oz/¼ cup) quick-cook polenta (cornmeal), whisking as you do so. Lower to a simmer and keep stirring until it reaches a smooth, creamy texture. Season with a little sea salt and freshly ground black pepper.

FOR THE TOASTED PINE NUTS

Toast 1 tbsp pine nuts in a dry frying pan until golden, shaking the pan every now and then.

FOR THE PURPLE SPROUTING BROCCOLI

Steam until cooked but still with a little bite.

TO ASSEMBLE YOUR BOWL

Spoon the coconut polenta into the base of the bowl, then add the laksa lamb and purple sprouting broccoli. Sprinkle over the toasted pine nuts and top with some very finely shredded spring onion (scallion) and green chilli.

HOT-SMOKED SALMON
CELERIAC REMOULADE
CUCUMBER RIBBONS
MIXED SALAD LEAVES
FARRO
NORI OLIVE OIL DRESSING

FOR THE CELERIAC REMOULADE

Peel and finely slice about ¼ medium celeriac (celery root), ideally with a mandolin. Slice again into thin strips and marinate in milk for a couple of hours. Drain and mix with some natural (plain) yogurt, 1 tsp horseradish mustard, a little sea salt, a squeeze of lime juice, and a couple of drops of Tabasco sauce.

FOR THE FARRO

Bring a pan of water to the boil and add a good pinch of sea salt and 55g (2oz/¼ cup) farro. Reduce the heat and simmer for about 30 minutes until cooked. Drain and mix with a little extra virgin olive oil.

FOR THE HOT-SMOKED SALMON

To smoke your own, rub a mixture of 1 part brown sugar and 1 part salt over a raw salmon fillet and dry-brine overnight in the refrigerator. Line the base of a stove-top smoker with equal amounts of uncooked rice and loose-leaf tea (Earl Grey or green are excellent) and place the grill rack over the tea and rice. Place, uncovered, on the hob over a medium heat until it starts to smoke. Rinse the brine off the salmon and place the fillet on the grill rack. Close the smoker with the cover, lower the heat, and smoke for 10–15 minutes, depending on how rare you prefer your salmon in the middle. Allow to cool a little (or you can serve cold) before flaking.

FOR THE CUCUMBER RIBBONS

Pare strips of cucumber, lengthways, using a swivel vegetable peeler. Season with a little sea salt and freshly ground black pepper.

TO ASSEMBLE YOUR BOWL

Spoon the farro into the bowl and add the celeriac remoulade and flaked salmon. Add the cucumber ribbons and a good handful of mixed salad leaves. Serve with a dressing of extra virgin olive oil infused with 1 tsp nori flakes.

COCONUT PRAWNS
PEAS
PEA SHOOTS
CONGEE RICE
SHREDDED HERBS

FOR THE CONGEE RICE

Put 100g (3½oz/½ cup) short-grain (or brown) rice, 850ml (3½ cups) water, a couple of thick slices of fresh ginger, and a bashed lemongrass stick into a saucepan. Bring to the boil, then reduce the heat to a low simmer for about 1 hour, or until the rice has completely broken down. Remove the ginger pieces and lemongrass.

FOR THE COCONUT PRAWNS

Marinate 85g (3oz/¾ cup) raw shelled prawns (shrimp) in 1 tbsp Thai green paste (see page 104) for 1 hour while the rice cooks. Heat 1 tsp sesame or groundnut (peanut) oil in a wok, add the prawns and then, after a couple of shakes of the wok, add 50ml (1¾fl oz/3½ tbsp) reduced-fat coconut milk. Cook the prawns until they turn pink.

FOR THE PEAS

Bring a small pan of water to the boil and add 85g (3oz/⅔ cup) peas (fresh or frozen). Cook for a minute or two, then drain.

TO ASSEMBLE YOUR BOWL

Add the congee rice to the bowl and then the prawns, peas, and a large handful of pea shoots. Scatter a few torn Thai basil leaves, coriander (cilantro) leaves, and shredded lime leaves over the top (optional). Mix it all through.

STORECUPBOARD RECIPES

BUTTERMILK DRESSING

Mix together 3 tbsp buttermilk, 1 tsp Dijon mustard, a splash of white balsamic vinegar, ½ finely chopped shallot, and 2 tbsp extra virgin olive oil. Season with sea salt to taste.

PRESERVED LEMON DRESSING

Mix together the finely chopped rind of 1 preserved lemon, 1 finely chopped shallot, ½ tsp coconut sugar, and a good pinch of sea salt. Add 1 part white wine vinegar to 3 parts extra virgin olive oil, to make a thick dressing.

TAHINI DRESSING

Mix together the juice of 1 lime, 1 tsp coconut sugar, 1 finely chopped garlic clove, 1 tbsp fish sauce, 1 heaped tbsp tahini, 1 tsp almond butter, and 1 tsp chilli oil, adding water as needed to give the desired consistency.

TURMERIC DRESSING

Mix together ½ tsp freshly grated or ground turmeric, 2 tsp pickled mustard seeds and the pickling liquid (see page 107), 1 tsp runny honey, and 3 tbsp extra virgin olive oil.

CITRUS-INFUSED OLIVE OIL

Place 500ml (17fl oz/2 cups) extra virgin olive oil in a pan with the pared zest of 1 lemon or orange. Gently warm for 5 minutes. Allow the oil to cool before transferring to an airtight jar with the zest.

CREOLE SPICE MIX

Mix together 1 tbsp crushed pink peppercorns, 6 crushed lime leaves or 1 tbsp grated lime zest, ¼ tsp garlic powder, ½ tsp ground ginger, and 1 tsp dried thyme leaves.

THAI GREEN PASTE

In a food processor, combine 50ml (1⅔fl oz/3½ tbsp) coconut cream, 1 tbsp coconut sugar, 2 green chilli peppers, 1 lemongrass stalk, ½ thumb-sized piece of ginger, peeled, zest and juice of 1 large or 2 small limes, 6 lime leaves (optional), ½ tsp grated fresh or ground turmeric, 1 tsp coriander seeds, and 1 tsp cumin seeds. Blitz to a paste. Store in an airtight jar in the refrigerator for up to 2 weeks.

LAKSA PASTE

Heat a dry frying pan (skillet) and add 1 tbsp coriander seeds, 1 tbsp cumin seeds, and 3 star anise. Toast for a minute or so until the aromas are released, then grind in a spice grinder or pestle and mortar. Add to a small food processor with 1 deseeded and chopped red chilli pepper, 55g (2oz/½ scant cup) peeled and roughly chopped fresh ginger, 8 lime leaves or the grated zest of 1 lime, 3 lemongrass stalks, and enough of a 1 part sesame oil to 1 part groundnut (peanut) oil mixture to form a smooth, quite thick paste when blitzed. Store in an airtight jar in the refrigerator for up to 1 month.

PICKLED RED ONION

Slice 1 or 2 red onions and blanch in boiling water. Drain and add to a pickling jar. Bring 100ml (3½fl oz/⅓ cup) apple cider vinegar and 50ml (1⅔fl oz/ 3½ tbsp) lemon or lime juice to the boil, add 1 heaped tbsp coconut sugar and 1 tsp mustard seeds. Stir until the sugar has dissolved. Pour over the sliced onions. Allow to cool to room temperature, then seal the lid. Store in an airtight jar in the refrigerator for up to 2 weeks.

KIMCHI

Shred the leaves of a Chinese cabbage and separate out the shreds. Toss in 1 tbsp sea salt, making sure the shreds are evenly covered, then leave to sit for a couple of hours before rinsing and draining. Mix together 40g (1½oz) Korean red pepper powder (gochugaru), 55g (2oz) anchovy sauce, and enough water to make a runny paste. Mix this with 1 tbsp grated fresh ginger, 1 crushed garlic clove, and a couple of sliced spring onions (scallions). Mix this into the cabbage, massaging the paste in well. Transfer to a sterilized jar so that there is a little liquid over the top of the cabbage. Seal and leave at room temperature for 1 day to kick-start the fermentation process, before storing in the refrigerator for up to 1 month. Open the lid every few days to relieve any pressure building up inside the jar.

PICKLED MUSTARD SEEDS

Heat 1 part apple cider vinegar to 2 parts water until boiling, then pour over mustard seeds in a pickling jar. Store in an airtight jar in the refrigerator for up to 1 month.

INDEX

The publisher would like to thank the following for the loan of bowls, spoons, and linens for photography:

PIP HARTLE

piphartle.com

DAISY COOPER

daisycooperceramics.com

TOM BUTCHER

tombutcherceramics.co.uk

KANA LONDON

kanalondon.com

HOPE IN THE WOODS

hopeinthewoods.com

SUE PRYKE

suepryke.com

NICK MEMBRY

kitchen-pottery.co.uk

ANDREA ROMAN

arceramics.co.uk

POTTERY WEST

potterywest.co.uk

ALEX DEVOL

woodwoven.com

THE LINEN WORKS

thelinenworks.co.uk